S.L.A.P. YOURSELF

(Selling Like a Professional Yourself)

BY

ELIJAH CUSHON

ISBN-13: 978-0692805046

ISBN-10: 0692805044

KIC Services Incorporated

Jefferson City, Missouri

This book is dedicated to you.

Table of Content

Introduction

Welcome to the Information Age. At this moment in time, we can share our experiences and knowledge with people all over the world right from our homes. I never would have known as a child the positive impact I could have on someone until I started sharing what I've learned about my career in sales. I truly believe that our experiences and information that comes with the time we invest in our careers will actually make a difference in our lives as well as the lives of others. That is why I share as much information as possible with others. To help make a difference.

Throughout the years I have dedicated to set myself and others up for success. Everyday, pursuing the American Dream. The"American Dream" I know was built upon hardworking men and woman who followed their purpose in life. What is your purpose in life? What is your dream? Following your purpose or dream involves changing yourself to be better than you were before- by honing in on a burning desire that stems from your core. Most know their purpose but forget that helping others is what it takes to fulfill that purpose. This is why I have so much passion in making others the best they can be in sales and other aspects of their life. Which is why I am going to share with you the secrets of how to S.L.A.P. (Sell Like A Professional) Yourself.

I remember growing up and starting to develop the life I wanted with my grandmother. I used to visit my grandmother at least twice a month. During this time she had me cut her grass every time. I was only excited to come over to eat her good cooking but she was building me up for so much more than I could ever imagine. I would wake up at 5:40 am to get the lawn mower ready and start cutting her grass. I would ask her why I had to do this and how much I was getting paid but she would ask, "You wanted money for school and to go out with your friends next week?" I would respond with '"Yes". She would say, "Well that's why you're cutting my grass." I didn't really understand back then. This was the worst thing you would expect to hear from a 45-year-old lady, especially as a preteen. I would still do whatever she asked, of course. She's my grandmother. Plus I wanted the money.

So after I was done I would put the lawnmower in the garage and go to her to collect my money. I wanted money for lunch when I was at school. Back then you could get some great snacks with as little as $2 per day. I asked her, "Why do I have to cut your lawn to get money?" She said, "You are investing in your future and that's what I'm helping you do." I asked, "What do you mean grandma." She said, "Invest in yourself so others won't have to invest in you, have goals and accomplish them." I then asked, "What does this have to do with cutting grass." She said, "I'm teaching you work ethics, if you want something then you have to work for it." This is something I will never forget. I always thought that some one should give me opportunities or money but I realized it was me that needed to create my own opportunities.

I remember back in 2010 I had dropped out of college and didn't know what I wanted to do with my life. All I knew is that college wasn't for me anymore but I wanted to make money to survive by paying my bills and buying food to contribute to the household. I lived with 2 roommates at the time and just moved back to Kansas City, Missouri from Lincoln University because I had just got out the R.O.T.C. program and couldn't afford to pay my tuition. I started hanging out with the wrong people, partying and put my focus in having fun instead of the dreams I wanted to accomplish. To sum it up I lost my motivation to do what was necessary to be successful.

Once I did make the initial move to Kansas City, I isolated myself to get my life back on track. I began to use the tools I learned from the 3 years I attended college. I sent out resumes and applied for jobs. In 2012 I came across an ad in my mothers living room that said' " Join the sales team of S&A Communications." I was very intrigued because it said, " You can make up to $600 a week". I knew that making $600 a week would allow me to pay my portion of rent, buy food without the assistance of welfare and eventually get me a car. A week later after making calls everyday to check on the status of my application I was granted an interview. That day I showed up in my best attire to make a great first impression. I followed the leading sales person in the field to get a feel of what the job description was about. That day we went door to door and knocked on about 17 doors and met about 8 new people. This experience changed the way I thought about how to survive to make ends meat. I realize that this company didn't wait for opportunity but took opportunity by the bulls horn to create its own. They sent people into communities and neighborhoods to sell their products and services. I only thought Jehovah witnesses went knocking at doors. I eventually was hired on in 48 hours which was the beginning of an experience that would take me further in the career of entrepreneurship and sales. I began to read books consistently to keep myself motivated and my mind fresh. During this time learned a lot about my strengths, weaknesses and how to work with others by using principles to accomplish personal and team goals. These basic principles gave me the opportunity to get a job working for a Fortune 500 company where I could further my endeavors in Corporate America.

I applied to work for AT&T in mid-Missouri in August of 2012. I traveled back to Jefferson City to stay with a fraternity brother. I stayed with him for a month and a half. I slept on his futon until offered an opportunity to work for the company. I didn't find out I was hired until one month being back in Jefferson City. I thank God for Orlando allowing me to stay at his apartment even though I did not have any money to pay him.

Once I began working for AT&T, I realized focusing on the trade of sales would get me far. School was honored by many but most I knew made less than 30,000 a year or couldn't find a job after getting their bachelors. I went from making less than 15,000 a year in 2011 to making more than 60,000 each year from 2013-2015.

This is why I wrote this book. To share information that will help others create their own opportunities in sales and other aspects of their life. I didn't know what I had to do to get to where I wanted to be, all I knew was something had to be done. In 2015, I started my own business called KIC Services Inc. which would be the foundation for helping small businesses market their products/services through a world renown networking community. The purpose is to teach skill sets and principles to bring them and their communities an abundance of economic and social stability.

Most of you have dreams and know the why behind it. You just don't know the how. Most importantly you don't embrace the motivation or drive that makes you go and get what you need to survive. That's what my grandmother tried to show me and Corporate America. This is what I'm going to show you in this book. How to S.L.A.P. (Sell

Like A Professional) Yourself and get the results you or your business need.

Have an open mind and learn some principles that you might not have learned anywhere else. I hope this book questions your thinking and your best practices in sales as well as life.

Chapter One

Purpose

Why are you here? What are you doing it for? What do you want out of life? Where do you see yourself 5-10 years from now? If money wasn't an issue what would you do with your life? What is your purpose? When you find this out don't forget it. Write it down and keep it with you. Make a vision board to remind yourself of your dreams everyday. This is your motivation. Use this motivation to capitalize on the opportunities you already have and those that will come throughout your journey.

I remember when working in retail I had a goal to be the best sales rep in the company. I was told that I could get paid a week of vacation for being the top 1% in the company. I also remember looking at the commission knowing that I could make more than $60,000 a year with this company. The whole reason I started with the company was to make money. I wanted to save this money to buy a car, pay off student loans and travel at leisure. These things motivated me because other people were already doing these things. I believe if someone else can do it then I can do it. I embedded these goals in my mind every day before I would start my day. Doing this created a burning desire that would allow me to achieve things that the naked eye could not see. The things I desired manifested into my life by believing in my dreams and applying myself.

I remember one day I went into work and I was in the middle of the rankings. Meaning I was halfway between the worst and best salesperson in the market. I'm talking about more than fifteen hundred people. It was the last month of the third quarter and I needed so many gross units to get to the top 5 spot in the region. That day I remember telling myself as I was driving to work, "I'm going to give it my all." I wanted to win a trip to California for me and my girlfriend. I mean this was a $4,500 trip at one of the best Resorts in Laguna Beach. I couldn't give that up. Also, I wanted to get a check over $4,000. I repeated over and over I would get 6 units that day. 5 hours into the day I was unable to close any deals. After time passed I was 5 pitches into the day. It was around 1:43pm. At this point I kept my motivation high by staying consistent with every customer and suddenly I closed a 25 unit deal which put me back into the top 1% of the region. I reminded myself daily why I continued to perform and gave it my all. I knew after that, embracing my dreams and staying motivated was the key to being successful in sales and in life.

People are motivated by different things. Once you find out what motivates you use that to light a burning desire to reach your dreams. Make the decision to be all the way in on your dreams by applying yourself to get what you desire. Have the "Whatever it takes mindset." This is difficult to do because it requires you to change your behaviors and sometimes putting yourself in uncomfortable situations. If you aren't uncomfortable then you're probably not doing "whatever it takes" to reach your dreams. Many things I've started in sales were uncomfortable until I became comfortable incorporating them consistently in my routine.

Sometimes it takes thinking outside of the box or maybe even doing things that others wouldn't do. I learned this by listening to others that were already successful in this field. You can learn by shadowing or being mentored by these people. They push your limits and help you reach your goals. In the long run you will be rewarded for doing whatever it takes (with having integrity and good ethics) to reach your dreams. Dream big!

Chapter Two

Positive attitude

Maintaining a positive attitude is a characteristic that influences how you feel everyday. Why? It changes how you react to situations as well as how others react to you. If you want to change your perception on situations you can change them by thinking positive. The truth is you have power over your attitude. No one else can control your attitude but you. Your attitude is one thing that will influence all the aspects of sales and your life. Don't worry about anything that you can't control, such as, other people's attitude.

We all know that one co-worker or friend who always has something negative to say about everything. These are the people who we dread to be around because they attempt to bring us down with them. Most likely you will not perform at your fullest potential, which, prevents you from reaching your goals. These are the people that you need not to associate with. They have a negative way of thinking. This does and will affect how you feel and how you performance. Why? Because you will be unmotivated to commit to your goals or dreams.

Essentially positive thinking stems from the way we think by finding the good in our circumstances. Once you began to approach situations with having a positive viewpoint, as well as being a problem solver, then you will see yourself beginning to increase in sales and the quality of life you will have. This way of thinking taught me to be mindful that business is business so don't take it personal. You should always control your temper. If you stay in honor, you will receive more profit for yourself and the company you work for.

Remember, people come in to work upset all the time, complaining about their issues and make it very uncomfortable to work with them. Make it a habit to stay positive by using the S. E. E. L. Factors. Smiling, maintaining eye contact, showing an abundance of enthusiasm and listening. Smiling has an enormous effect on others especially their perception of you. Even if you are not happy, smiling will have others assuming that you are happy. It also puts those around you in a good mood. The truth is all we want is to feel good and be around others that put us in a good mood.

Also give others eye contact when you are in conversation. Doing this displays a level of respect you have for others and keeps their attention. This non-verbal communication will be perceived as being positive. Everyone wants to be around others who have positive energy.

Isaac Newton said "Energy is neither created nor destroyed only transferred". This energy in sales is your attitude which is displayed through your enthusiasm . How often do you get excited about things?

Do you enjoy helping others or solving other people problems? Consistently keep a positive attitude by showing it (smiling) or saying such as: we will figure it out together. Think about what you can do that to put them in a good mood?

Fourth is listening. To understand peoples problems fully and find a suitable solution for them you have to really listen to what they are saying. Retain the information they give you. Sometimes repeat back what someone has said so they know you're actually listening to them. This puts you in a position to actually offer solutions and sell the products that you offer. If you do this consistently you will see a difference in the results you aim to achieve.

Do you have the power to control your actions and the way you respond to others? Yes, but it comes with keeping a positive attitude and having a positive thinking process. A great way to respond is with positive affirmation such as, making positive statements when solving problems. The truth is others will make negative comments but you being positive, will keep you and possibly them in a good mood. Say comments like, "We will figure this out", "I'm glad you brought this to my attention", or "Lets look at some options", will be very impactful. It will put you in a positive mindset and get others to think that way as well.

Use an acronym called A.E.R.R. This stands for Acknowledge, Empathize and Resume/Reassure. This is very useful when dealing with people who are upset or previously had a bad experience with your product. It's important to make them feel as if their issue is the most important thing in the world. Really it's just us listening and responding positively.

First, Acknowledge their issue. Acknowledging their issue shows them you recognize the problem and that it's important to you and the company. Second, empathize with them. Empathizing is putting yourself in their shoes. If you think about it there is no reason why you shouldn't be open minded to your customer's viewpoint. You've been in their shoes once before. Third reassure them that you will take ownership. Reassuring is giving them confirmation that you recognized the problem and are willing to resolve it. Resume after listening to their concerns by continuing on the sales process. This works no matter what situation you come across. Continue with the conversation where you intended for it to go. This is how you control the sale. Your AER statements will be impactful in gaining trust as well as controlling the conversation. Don't be afraid to Acknowledge, Empathize, Reassure and Resume in you conversations.

Chapter Three

Enthusiasm

People buy into excitement no matter their background, culture, business, political preference or nationality. The concept of enthusiasm is to use all of your positive energy to influence others in an uplifting way. Essentially it's the transfer of positive energy from one person to another person or a group of people through excitement. You can master this characteristic by genuinely enjoying what you do.

I have always been an excited or over the top type of guy. I love getting pumped up at every event and continuing to surround myself with others that generally enjoy life or having fun. I remember while in college being able to submerge myself into many organizations that had the image of having fun and promoting their events throughout campus. No matter how big or small the event the excitement these students exhibited could have made you believe that they were having the best events on campus.

When I joined The National Society of Pershing Rifles I was able to surround myself with others that understood the principle of enthusiasm and its effect on results. This was the first time I heard something that I will never forget: "Enthusiasm is like a catalyst. When added to wisdom and experience it will produce small miracles." As I went through my military training process with this organization. Having fun was the key factor in making long weeks feel as if they were mere days. They pushed my mental capacity and physical training to its limit.

This concept continues to work for me this day. I worked for a corporation for years taking on 8-10 hour shifts for 5-6 days a week. These long hours will fatigue you physically and mentally if you allow it to. So I would turn to things like music, friends, books, audio tapes or even entertainment to uplift my spirit. These gave me motivation to perform in order to get the results I wanted. If you use these resources consistently like I did such as music, friends, books and etc. you will be able to take that energy and use it in your sales pitch every day to capitalize on opportunities. That enthusiasm you display will have a great influence on that person's decision to buy your product.

Chapter Four

Confidence

Confidence is key to anything that you do or aspire to accomplish. "Confidence is the belief in oneself, one's powers or one's abilities-dictionary.com. The question isn't , "can I do this?" The question is, "Do I believe that I can do this?" Ask yourself this before getting in sales or any profession. You have to BELIEVE that you can do the task at hand and excel in it. Even if you have never tried doing it before. Having this confidence is sure to give you the mindset that no matter what obstacles get in the way you will persevere through them. Confidence is a characteristic that is developed through time, experience and having people around you that encourage you everyday. I've been honored to encounter a diverse group of leaders in corporate America and college that build my confidence. They encouraged me throughout my journey so I can reach my goals. I honestly believe that this is the most crucial part in gaining confidence. There is nothing worse than being surrounded around those who diminish your confidence with negativity. I've experienced working with colleagues who discouraged me by saying, "it can't be done" or "I won't be able to do it."

In 2011 when I worked door to door in sales we were on our way to the the North Kansas City Area. I was being trained to sell home services. As we walked I met many people in many communities. The person training me was unable to close any offers. As the day went by, she started to make comments like "This is a tough job and you won't make a lot of money doing this. " She said, "If you're lucky enough to sign up one person then you had a good day." A few days later I went off on my own knocking door to door selling and closed 4 deals in one day. Everything she said about not being able to close more than one in a day — I proved wrong. That same day when we got back in the office and let the owner know what we accomplished, my trainer said, "he just had a lucky day so we won't expect this to happen all the time". That comment had crushed my spirit. In actuality she was bringing me down because of her own circumstances and disbelief in herself. At that moment I had lost respect for her and her discouraging statements made me not want to work with her.

These people are every where. They don't want to see you achieve your dreams. Don't let these people get to you. On the other hand I have experienced working with others who continuously build my confidence level. In 2013 working in Jefferson City, Mo I worked with leaders who would constantly praise me for hitting my goals. My mentor, Eric, would constantly give me high fives with encouraging statements saying "Elijah you can do it." or "I'm proud of what your doing." Eric made sure to speak positively to build my confidence level by merely telling me I could do it every day and praised me for my accomplish-ments. This changed my view on how impactful positive people can influence how you feel about yourself.

Chapter Five

What's Your Brand?

What brand do you represent? How will you be perceived by your audience? Branding is everything with selling your product. Branding starts with first impression. Whether we realize it or not, we are the products that we sell. Customers come to us for a product and we attach ourselves with the products we offer.

So what is your image? Do you look presentable in the profession that you are in. I consistently dressed business casual and sometimes business suits because customers respected me as a professional. More importantly they associate that image with comfort and trustworthiness. Is your attire clean? Make sure to keep your clothing wrinkle free without any stains. What about shoes? Do your shoes match your clothing? Make sure to wear dress shoes with dress attire and socks that are appropriate with them. Even a blazer with dress shoes to show that you mean business and make the customer comfortable working with you.

Consistently keep your hygiene up to par. Making sure that you have a clean shave for the business you represent. Some allow tattoos to be worn but it depends on the business you represent. Maybe the audience you serve doesn't feel comfortable working with people that have tattoos showing all over their body. So you might want to wear long sleeves if you have tattoos on your arms. The first impression is simply what the customer sees and the next is what they hear. Speak professionally without using slang or derogatory words when working with people. If you would feel indifferent about going into an establishment or someone's home using certain terms then its important to respect others in the same manner. Something I learned throughout my career is to be able to adapt and read people.

Most can't do this but there are a few people who naturally possess this talent. Learn how to read peoples body language very well.

Most importantly your character as a person and a leader will define your brand. This was something that was difficult for me at first but with the right mentoring I was able to be developed into a better person and a leader for others. Mentors such as business owners, teachers, and friends. These are the people I call leaders in my life. They not only say what they do but do what they say. Observe and watch what people do to determine if they are good leaders. Your actions as a follower or a leader will show your true brand.

Again, what customers see first is the image, then they hear what you say, and last they watch what you do. Keep these factors in mind when building your brand for yourself and the company that you represent. Remember you're just not representing yourself. You are repre-senting others who put their name on the line for such as: businesses, family, friends, mentors and many others you haven't met yet.

Doing these things will build your brand to become an effective communicator, solution provider and sales person.

Chapter Six

Developing People Skills

This is something that should be a personal goal for any and everyone. In order to increase your net worth you need to increase your network. Talking to people is something most people struggle with because it can be very uncomfortable to interact with strangers. But remember a stranger is a friend you haven't met yet.

Organizations in college helped me to develop interpersonal relationship skills. We would have events that would give us the opportunity to meet people. This would be significant in growing my network. Also, while working for a Fortune 500 company, when invited to conventions or seminars, I would go just to meet new people. These were opportunities that most people missed out on because they think it's a bunch of people listening to lectures. Yes, you learn a lot from the lectures but for me it was the total opposite.

I was able to meet others who were very successful and influential in their positions from all over the country. These were the people that would connect me to the opportunities I was looking for in my career. They would be difficult to come in contact with during my day to day lifestyle because I worked 40 hours per week while raising my sons. Also these organizations give you the opportunity to meet people you wouldn't meet in your personal life. Why? You come together for a common purpose bigger than yourself. Getting to know these people will build a solid relationship where you can reach out for advice, favors or resources you don't have. This is huge for getting to your dreams and goals.

How do you get to this point? How do you develop your people skills? First step is respect. Always treat people with respect and treat them the way you want to be treated. Always talk to people the way you would want them to talk to you. Be understanding and listen. This brings me to my second point in developing people skills, Listen! Do this as much as possible. Everyone likes a good listener. Listening gives you the opportunity to learn something or discover opportunities. People tell you valuable information all the time but you miss out on them because you are not an effective listener. Others tell you what they like, their goals, and even the problems they face in life. All you have to do is listen and ask the right questions.

Asking the right questions is also a great way to develop people skills. Like I said, people love talking about themselves and want someone to listen to them; especially when they are telling their stories. I love asking people about their stories. It's like opening Pandora's box.

It's a great starter question when meeting new people. When people tell their stories they are opening themselves up to you. So in return you have to be genuine in receiving this information . Connect with them by finding what you have in common. The goal is to make them your friend. Once you share common interest and you get to know them personally you are well on your way to building your network. Remember that developing peoples skills is something that happens with time and practice. Just get out there and meet new people.

Chapter Seven

Make A Plan

The first part of making a plan is having a goal. A goal can be something you expect to accomplish within one month or maybe 5 years from now. Plans usually stem from a dream. For example: After graduation in 2007, I wanted a Mustang. I remember when I first saw my friend's dad drop him off in a mustang at school. I went up to his car as I gazed up on its beautiful red paint. The body was sure to get looks and the engine sounded as smooth as the winds section in a band. I asked him how do I get one of these he said you have to plan on getting it and save to get it.

There are 8 steps in making a plan. First, If you want a 2007 convertible Ford Mustang with a 5 speed stick shift then you have to know how much it cost.

Second, If it costs $7,500 then you have to figure out how you're going to get that money.

Third, If you decide to sell a product or service to get money, then you're going to have to create a deadline and specified actions to get the funds for the Mustang. You create action steps to lead you to the goals you want to accomplish. I try to be as specific as possible with my plan of action by writing the when, how, where and why.

Fourth, Make a contact list of your prospective customers or clients. This list will consist of family, friends, colleagues, businesses, organizations and much more. This is your current network of people you have already build a relationships with. They will then help by purchasing or referring your business to their network. This is one of the most crucial parts of the plan.

Fifth, find out who you need to involve to get the job done. These people will be very important with giving input such as critical feedback and performing tasks that need to be done. I had my coach, Scott Chapman, help me create plans to maximize my sales check. Amber Davis helped me save money to get a car by holding me accountable. Tyrone Flowers assisted me with branding my image. These people are subject matter experts in areas that I struggled in.

Sixth, Make sure to create a timeline for achieving your goal. Mark dates down and commit to taking action. Most importantly write down how the task will be completed. Knowing how to get the job done gives you confidence to actually take action. If you know how to complete the task then eventually you will make progress towards your goal as long as you commit to it.

The seventh step is to track your progress. Tracking it will show you what's working and what's not. I can tell what's working based on what the numbers are telling me. especially my profit gains. If you want to sell 20 units in a week then track what each customer purchased. How many you sold in one day and what made them purchase the product will give insight on how to maximize on your audience. I want to know which products I sold and how much I profited by selling the product.

The Last step is to save or invest. Decide how much of that money is going into your savings and how much is going back into your business. Essentially manage your finances and accounting.

Once I have followed these steps then I revisit the plan and the progress I've made thus far. I'm either going to be satisfied with my results or disappointed. I actually was able to save for a Mustang. I had over $8,000 in cash ready to buy it whenever I wanted it.

There will be obstacles and failures during this process but you have to decide if you want to continue following the same action steps or revise them but not change the goal. If I decide to change my action steps I usually reach out to my mentors for best practices and incorporate them into my plan. I go over that new plan with my mentors and follow through with them and start the cycle over again. Follow these steps you will get the results you want and more importantly the dreams that you desire.

Chapter Eight

Know Your Customer

In order to give your product value you have to get to know your customer. There is something called 80/20 rule. If you master this you will be on your way to connecting the product to the customer, which will get them to buy it. The 80/20 rules is where the customer should talk 80% of the time and you 20%. The key factor is getting the customer to feel comfortable so that they will open up to you. Ask open-ended questions to give you enough information to qualify them for a product or service. In sales I have witnessed a lot of failed attempts to uncover information due to representatives asking closed ended questions. Closed questions will give you a yes or no response.

Open ended questions will get your customer to respond with a statement. Like I said before people love talking about themselves. I would suggest starting off with How, what, when, who at the beginning of your sentences. This will assist you in asking open-ended questions. I've had great success with gearing questions around an acronym called F.O.R.D.S. that stands for family, occupation, recreation, dogs, story. Such as: tell me about your family? what do you do for a living? What does your family do for fun? What kind of pets do you have? What's your story? These are just starter questions that should lead to follow up questions. Uncovering this information will be very successful to find common interests that you and the customer or client share.

Don't sell yourself short either. Ask follow up questions to dig a little deeper into topics that most interest the customer. If the customer likes sports talk about sports; follow up with a question that's geared around the type of sports they like and their favorite teams. If you find out what they do for living follow up by asking how they got into their field. Again, talk about what the customer likes. This gets them to trust you a little more. Gaining their trust is the whole objective to getting to know them. This information you uncover will be used to actually tie back a personalized solution for the product or services you offer. During this step you should make a friend.

Casual conversation and small talk are sure to build rapport with a customer as well. Casual talk is questions such as, what do you have planned for today, so where are you from, what kind of vacation you have planned this year. These questions just keep the conversation going. It's easier to offer solutions to friends because there is some form of trust built. Why? Because friends have common interest or things that bind them together. This is your goal, to find out what binds you and the customer. If you do this most will buy from you because you listened to them and they now trust you. I've bought from people because I felt like we knew each other or better yet they knew me by listening to me. People will do the same for you. If you will create friends during the sales process by getting to know them they are more likely to buy your products.

Chapter Nine

Know Your Product or Service

Do you get frustrated when you go into a store and you ask a representative about a product and he/she knows nothing about it? First thing that comes to my mind is , "why did they hire this person" or "I could have gone online?". Most customers leave and go to another competitor to make the purchase. Not knowing your product will prevent your from being a successful sales person.

The first step is to research everything that you can about the product you offer. Why? Doing this will give you confidence when offering the product as a solution. If you don't know the product you can't convince anyone to buy it. Make sure to study the benefits of the products for the company you work for. People will trust you more when you can state the facts and display that you know a lot about the products you offer. Not only knowing what products you offer but knowing why it would benefit the customer will close the sale. Doing this will close more offers because you can respond to questions without long pauses. Its very awkward when a potential buyer asks you about a product and you don't have the information. The customer's perception is that you're not credible. I recommend taking 20 minutes a day for 4 days minimum to study the products you offer. Also study your competitors in the market. Knowing what products you are competing against will give you the opportunity to give the client or customer your product advantages in the markets.

Most importantly buy your products and use them. I don't know anyone who doesn't like to use new products. You will have more en-thusiasm when offering products if you use them. I figured out that when you use the products you sell, you become comfortable talking about them. I was comfortable because my confidence level went up. Using the product increases your knowledge of the product, which makes you feel empowered. That's how I view confidence, as a feeling of empowerment. You will want to share your experiences about using the product and want customers to have the same experience that you have. The customer will also buy a product that someone else is using because the customer wants to know their experience with the prod-uct. If you continue to use the product then the product has built more credibility to be used. If others aren't using it then the customer will not believe it is worth purchasing. Use your products and services that you offer.

Chapter Ten

Offer problem solving solutions (OPS)

Do you believe that your product can solve problems? Have you tested the product to know that it gets the job done that people need? Can you give a testimonial of how the product changed your life? You have to know your product and believe in it. If you don't believe in it then you won't be confident when offering the product. How can this product offer a valuable solution to someone? Well first there has to be a need for your prospective buyer. It's up to you to find why they need it. Without uncovering that need for the product then it's going to be difficult to get the customer to buy the product.

After you get to know the customer you can finally offer them a solution. You want to offer one complete solution with one price. You should never offer a price until you have found out your customers needs and demonstrated each product to the customer. This will make you very successful with closing any offer. Demonstrating your product whenever you can is going to increase your close rates. Close rate is how many customers you offered your product to as the denominator and how many actually bought the product as the numerator. Also, you should always have your product available to demonstrate. If it's a video then have it available to show through your tablet, laptop etc. If it's a tangible product then keep it with you every where you go. If it's business cards don't leave the house with out them.

At any moment a potential buyer could be the difference in closing offers or missing opportunities. Why? You want to put some tangible product in the customers hands. This gives the buyer a visual of the product of what you can do for them or what the product can do for them. People buy more when the product is on hand or in stock. We live in an instant gratification society with impulse buyers. When you demo the product It brings the experience to life in front of their eyes. Hence the term. "You have to see it to believe it". Also say that the offer doesn't close. The feeling of having brochure, flyer or business card will be a reminder for them to give it a second thought. When showing the product give your pitch.

Every contact you have with someone is a potential buyer. So you should offer the products you sell. Don't just show a product and not explain why it benefits the customer. I usually give at least 2-3 reasons why the customer should purchase the product today. If you don't offer it or show it then they won't buy it.

This is one reason why many are unsuccessful in sales. They won't offer the product because they are afraid of hearing "No", but your going to hear many "No's" before you get a "Yes" no matter how great the product is. Build the courage to get out there and sell your product. You can sell it if you offer it. Somebody will buy it if you give them the opportunity and every contact is an opportunity for a sale. If the offer makes sense for the customer tell them. Example: "Hey, John this makes sense for you because you said......", now fill in the rest. Tell them what they told you. This is how you tie the product back to them. It's a no brainier.

This is offering problem solving solutions. Show excitement when offering your products. People want to know that you believe in the product that you are offering. Example: "Hey John, i want to show you something amazing, I know you will love this." Or "This is something I know you don't want to miss out on".

Chapter Eleven

Close the Offer

Close the offer by getting the person to agree to purchase the product. This is the whole objective of sales. When the customer buys every one wins, the customer the company and yourself. It's a 3 for one deal and everyone is happy at the end. Remember that the customer is gaining for purchasing the product or missing out if they don't and you have to genuinely believe that.

These are some of the things I say to close the offer:

Let's do it today!

What's holding you back?

This is how we can get started.

How would you like to pay?

Sometimes you do not close the offer the first time you offer it. This is when you have to recap why the product makes sense for them. You do this by using what you uncovered and personalize the solution for the customer. For example:

"Hey (name) you stated that.....this is why the product makes sense for you.....you have nothing to lose. You should have at least 2 response statements to overcome objections. Sometimes you might have to build more rapport by getting to know them a little more. Be as genuine as possible. Forget that you are even selling the product for a while. Just enjoy having a conversation and making a friend to network with. If you do not close the offer its crucial that you don't make it a big deal.

Tip: Use the fear of losing a deal in their mind. If you say, "Now is the time to do it" or, "This is a limited time offer". You're insinuating to them that it's a once in a life time opportunity. Remember, you have to be convincing by saying it with conviction. If you don't believe it no one else will.

Chapter Twelve

"No" Big deal!

It's ok to say it to the customer genuinely, "Hey (name) it's not a big deal. I know this offer really made sense for you but here's a few of my cards. If you know any one that this might benefit please let me know." Do this and move on to the next opportunity. I have come to realize that what we do is difficult at times. Why is it difficult? Because this trade comes with more failures than successes that most can't endure. What is it? The word "No" and a customer's decision not to purchase. I've had my fair share of hearing the word "No" 80 % of the time in retail sales. This word separates the winners from the quitters. Once you are able to overcome the word "No", which is just an obstacle to overcome, then you are well on your way to achieving your goals. Like I stated in the previous chapter, closing the offer is important for the business and achieving the results you want, but sometimes you will not close the offer. That's just that.

We get so focused on closing offers that we forget what it takes to close offers. In order to close you have to hear the word "No". That doesn't mean it's the end of the world or you won't hit the goals you're aiming for. It just means you haven't met the right buyer. Especially if you follow the process it takes to close sales. I've had days in retail where I worked from 8am to 8pm. Some days I wasn't able to close an offer until 7pm or after close. This was only possible because I trusted the sales system. I knew, trusting in the law of averages, I would eventually close offers.

I did door to door sales for about 5 months. Door to door is one of the most difficult and defining moments for people and their future in sales. If you can succeed at door to door then you can sale for any company at any level. We worked 6 days a week and only got paid on commission. The first day by myself I had 35 doors to knock on over and over until someone answered. Maybe 15 people answered their door. I was able to pitch 7 offers. I closed 4 of the offers. This happened because I didn't give up throughout the day. Staying positive as I made my rounds to each prospective buyer. Even though I was only able to pitch 15 out of 35 opportunities and closed 4 out of 15 pitches I didn't allow it to affect my performance.

I accepted the fact that I had something bigger to work for (at that moment a car and rent). So I kept on knocking at doors even though I would hear "No" 75% of the time. How did I get through that time? Easy, "No big deal". That's what I told myself all the time. It's not a big deal and I still believe that to this day. Anything that's not in my control I don't worry about it. Only worry about the things you can control because that's the deciding factor in everything. Why? Because it's No

Big Deal.

Chapter Thirteen

Recap, Reassure and Ask for Referrals

When you have already closed the offer with the customer you want to close out the interaction strong. Recap what you and the customer went over and reassure them that they have made the right decision. Customers appreciate you doing this. It shows that you are genuine about what you do. Most customers are impulsive buyers and sometimes leave questioning their decision; this is called buyer's remorse. We have all had buyer's remorse sometime in our life and some of us have buyer's remorse all of the time. The question is how do you prevent your customer from having buyers remorse?

First you want to recap the offer and while recapping the offer remind them why they decided to buy it. Example: "Hey, Mr. Customer this is what we did today ... and I reassure you that this will...". Reassuring them that they made the best decision by pointing out how it was personalized to solve a problem for them will be critical before ending the interaction. The goal is to have the customer excited about making the right purchase.

Think about a time you made a purchase that you were excited about. What did you do? You probably told all your friends and family about it. That's what people do when they buy something new. They become walking advertisements. This is why it's important to hand out at least 3 business cards and ask for referrals. Anyone who enjoyed their buying experience and the products they purchased will tell others about it. What does it do for you? It grows your business and customer base. Let others do the work that you don't have to. Promote your service and your products by reference.

Also I get their information like email, phone number or social media pages. I use any platform that I can to contact them and thank them for their time. I always show my customers appreciation. Time is very important to all of us. Tell the customer, " I appreciate you for your time and business". Saying this will definitely leave a lasting impression.

Chapter Fourteen

Follow Up

The most crucial step in sales and customer service is to follow up with your clients. This step is for three main purposes, which include feedback, up-selling, and getting referrals. What you will find out is that most consumers will talk about their experience with the products they purchase and how they were treated. You getting this information from your client will help you get better in selling. Also it will show them that you actually care about their previous experience.

Up-selling is another reason to follow-up with the customer. This is a consumer world. People like to buy, shop, and spend their money. The customer or client is busy just like you are every day. They might not know what other products you have to offer or maybe they forgot about coming back in to buy something they committed to previously. It is your job to remind them in the most effective way to come back and purchase when you follow up with them. This is where you will get a significant amount of sales.

Getting referrals is what we want with every customer that we have. It's your job to give the customer the best experience by leaving a last-ing impression on them. The transaction should be fun and make them feel good afterwards. When you contact the customer back you want to ask did they get everything they needed and if they need any more assistance to contact you. This will keep you and the company in their head. What other companies actually follow up. Many companies are getting to understand that with the internet and so many other options to buy that they have to start personalizing their relationships with customers. This is what gets the referrals because they will tell their family and friends about the experience they had with you.

There are different ways that you can follow up with a customers. Many will include but not limited are email, phone call, writing a letter, text messaging, social media or showing up in your persons. Use a few if not all of these methods to get the feed back you need to improve the customers experience, up-sell and to get referrals. Take time out of your day every day to follow up with your clients or make a day out the week that you follow up with all of your clients.

Chapter Fifteen

Ownership

What is ownership exactly? Ownership is the act, state, or right of possessing something. How does this apply to sales? How does it apply to our everyday life? Well first you need to understand the opposite of ownership which is excuses. What are excuses? Excuses are tools of incompetence that seldom lead to anywhere or no where at all.

First, using excuses to avoid ownership of a problem is a huge mistake. I used to have excuses such as "I forgot all about it" or " it's not my fault". You want to avoid using these type of statements because it gives the perception that your not owning up to your mistakes. I also remember being at work and not wanting to be there. So I wouldn't offer products or give the customer the world class buying experience they deserved. Maybe I wasn't having a good day or I wasn't motivated. Making and excepting excuses will prevent you from hitting your goals. Excuses prevented me from making an extra $400 a month at one point. Really I was making up excuses to avoid taking ownership of my laziness. In the long run I missed out on making money and the customer missed out on making their life better or easier with our products. So excuses are a characteristic of laziness. Being lazy will bring you regret in the long run.

Second, avoiding ownership by not overcoming your fears. Especially the fear of rejection when offering products. Sometimes we get complacent with our results without taking ownership to change them. This prevents you from working hard on a daily basis. Instead you should do what ever it takes to change your circumstance to have that sense of control over your life. Failing is easier than being successful and if you want the easy way out keep on giving excuses. But you will not be rewarded in the long run.

Want to be rewarded? Take ownership of your circumstances. Leaders and those who are self-sufficient take ownership of their circumstances or problem. Build up the courage to tackle problems and own your circumstances so you can find a solution to solve problems for yourself and others.

A few things I would recommend to do is to have a positive mindset first. Ask yourself, How can I fix this issue? What can I do differently to change the outcome? Statements like these changes the way you act. Taking ownership starts with our thinking process and how we react to our circumstances. If you want to be successful then take ownership, doing this will take you down the path of success like it did for me.

Chapter Sixteen

Patience is Key

In order to build trust with people when you're in the business of sales, you have to be patient with customers. Many of your sales come from those who might have a lot of questions about your product or services. In order to respond effectively you have to listen to their concerns and answer them with competence. Listening is overall the focus of gaining their trust to offer a solution. After listening to them the next step is to offer a problem solving solution. Sometimes solving an issue for the customer can be very tedious. There always seem to be many obstacles that arise when trying find a solution. These problems vary from technical issues, needing to do more research or even getting the customer to cooperate. I've learned that if you stay positive while being patient with the process then everything seems to workout.

I remember working with a customer who had a billing issue that was higher than normal. They we're really upset about it because they felt lied to by a previous representative. I listened to their concerns and recapped everything they told me (AERR). I then reassured them that we would get it figured out together. After doing further research I realized that I needed help from management. It took us about 30min to find the solution for the customer being placed on an incorrect plan they did not agree to. After discovering the problem, I thanked them for their patience and fixed the issue by taking ownership of problem. The lady was reimbursed but still wanted to rant about how she was mistreated. I continued to listen as I thanked her for her business for about 10 more minutes. Once she was done I discovered that she needed services for her children and was able to make more money by up-selling her the products that were not offered to her by the first representative.

At this moment I knew that continuing to stay patient by helping the customer and listening to her allowed me to gain her trust.

Sometimes being patient with people and listening to them will allow you to have more opportunities to sell your products and services. How? Because you do everything you can to service the customer by going above and beyond. There is nothing that you shouldn't do to provide the best service and experience that you have to offer.

Chapter Seventeen

Don't Give Up

If you use these principles in your everyday sales or on your entrepreneurial journey. I know that you will reach your dreams. Iv'e been using these steps throughout my career in sales and on my road to running my own business. They've given me the positive results I've been wanting and will do the same for you. I want to reiterate that you have to keep a positive attitude because you will experience hardship on your journey. Keep positive thinking people around you as much as possible to keep you going. Surround yourself with those who believe in you. Don't give up on yourself because your time is now. There will be obstacles that get in your way but you can and will overcome them. I believe you can do it. Maximize your potential in sales. Maximize your time you have to impact others. Your time is now. S.L.A.P. (Sell Like a Professional) Yourself like never before and watch your dreams come true. Remember " Don't Give Up".

www.ingramcontent.com/pod-product-compliance
Lightning Source LLC
Chambersburg PA
CBHW032019190326
41520CB00007B/537